MW01106809

ISBN 978-1-54398-656-3
This edition published in 2019
© 2019 SheWorth Inc.

Welcome!

We are so excited for you to begin your path to worthiness.
Let this journal serve as a daily reminder that you are worthy
and deserving of this journey.

With much love,

SheWorth

** Athena, the Ancient Greek goddess of strength and wisdom is represented
throughout this Journal and is an icon for the SheWorth movement. Every single
woman is a goddess in her own right and we want to encourage women to step into
their strength, wisdom, power, and inner warrior.*

Table of Contents

Rewiring the brain is the secret to change. Small steps toward self reflection lead you closer to the person you are meant to be.

Erica Spiegelman
Rewired

About SheWorth

SheWorth aspires to be a place for women to share their stories, understand themselves and create positive change. SheWorth is curated by strong women who have had their own "Brave Moments," and have been inspired to share what they have learned with all women who have parallel experiences. The principles and resources provided in this journal and all things SheWorth, have been curated by a Professional Psychologist. We want this movement to be more than "positive thinking" (which is great!), but also real, evidence and science-based strategies to help propel women forward.

SheWorth is a movement meant to inspire, motivate and cultivate change. In a post #MeToo world, we are on the cusp of the most significant women's movement: a fourth wave of feminism which will propel women forward. SheWorth will provide scientific-based strategies, articles, and expertise aimed at promoting self-worth, improving mental health, and ultimately changing the world! Women have come a long way, but we have a long way to go. There is a groundswell of awareness around women's incredible power, but it has to start with women themselves, believing in their own strength and ultimate **SheWorth**!!!

www.sheworth.org
IG: sheworth_women
Twitter: @WorthShe

The most difficult thing is the decision to act, the rest is merely tenacity.

Amelia Earhart

What to Expect

The exclusive SheWorth Journal is an evidence-based healing and motivational system that will ensure you become a braver, happier, and more confident version of yourself. The SheWorth movement is a women's empowerment movement. We believe that every single woman has had her own version of a brave moment throughout her lifetime. Brave moments may include things like: finishing college, leaving an abusive relationship, completing a challenging race, caring for a loved one, or even just getting out of bed in the morning and facing another day.

The SheWorth Journal unapologetically aspires to move women toward the goals and versions of themselves that they want to be.

Saying no to others means saying yes to yourself.

Introduction

Research on behavioral change shows that repetition is one of the most effective ways for the brain to learn. If we continually challenge ourselves with intentionality, over time- our brains will change. It is a fascinating process known as "neuroplasticity." When your brain is repeatedly exposed to particular people, places, or things, the brain changes in response (for better or worse!) to these situations. This journal is about helping you become the best version of yourself. Change your brain by setting small, attainable goals, achieving them, and celebrating your success! This in turn leads to a surge in dopamine, a happy brain chemical, which you can build on!!

The SheWorth Journal will also challenge you to reflect on the relationships and scenarios in your life that may not be serving you. There is something in neuroscience known as "mirror neurons" and it essentially means that- those that we hang around have a big impact! We begin to "mirror" behaviors, emotions, and thoughts of the people that we spend the most time with. Therefore, think about the people you spend your time with, your precious, beautiful time! We want to challenge you to think about people and scenarios that you may need to set boundaries around, so that you can be free to tap into your TRUE WORTHINESS.

Date _3 November_

A.M. _How do you feel right now?_ ○○○○○○✗○○○
Good   _Not Good_

Stayed up late for work

Today I commit to...

- Going for my morning run
- Putting everything down when my mom comes
over to visit and truly listen to her
- Pausing and checking in with my breath

The affirmation I will repeat to myself today is...

I am the most positive person I know.

Because I am worthy, I will...

Give myself one hour in the evening and do
whatever my heart desires.

How to Use

The SheWorth Journal is your own personal place to gather inspiration and challenge yourself toward growth and healing. We recommend that you commit to using the journal daily, for 30 days. The journal is laid out in four sections.

Section 1: Education
The first section explains how to use the Journal, provides examples, and lays out the Psychology and Science behind why the recommendations in this journal are effective.

Section 2: The Heart of the Journal.
This is where you will spend most of your time. It is undated, so that if you miss a day- it's no big deal. The entry provides an AM and PM page with three questions to ponder. This section will help you visualize, internalize, and move toward the best, most worthy version of yourself!

Section 3: Creative Mind Wandering Space
The final section is a place to "dream," with more white space and open-ended questions for you to brainstorm and jot down longer-term goals.

Section 4: Random Musings
Dedicated lined journal space for you to use as you wish. Remember: The act of putting pen to paper can help you to clarify your thoughts and emotions. ♥

P.M. *How do you feel right now?* ○ⓧ○○○○○○○○
                                    Good   *Not Good*

Had dinner with old friend

What is one thing that went well today...

I didn't rush the morning routine with the kids
I was present & listening with intent

Today, I am proud that I...

Went for a run and worked on a project that
   meant a lot to me

Tomorrow, I hope to...

Continue to be positive and patient with myself
and my family

ⓧ *I told myself that I was worthy today.*

How to Use (continued)

We recommend that you check in with your journal daily, but we have intentionally left the date open-ended so that you can personalize it and use it in a way that works best for you! The Journal has 30 days' worth of content.

Research shows that meaningful progress can happen for individuals with repetition and persistence. Imagine where you could be if you committed to reflecting on yourself, getting quiet, and tuning in to your inner worthiness for just 30 days. As you grow and evolve, the journal will grow and evolve with you. Take the time to read Section 1, and then get started TODAY on Section 2. You got this!

Section 1
Education

A brief overview of evidence-based principles drawn from the fields of Cognitive Neuroscience, Positive Psychology, Behavior Change, and Evolutionary Psychology.

If not for yourself,
then who?
If not now, then when?

Neuroplasticity

Our brain is the area that in many ways "masterminds it all." It sends out chemical messages via electrical impulses to inform our emotions, choices, thoughts, and behaviors. The brain changes in response to our environment. The people we hang out with, the self-talk we engage in, and the environmental cues we are exposed to everyday truly do matter. A very basic understanding of how the brain processes information and deals with experiences is so valuable.

Neuroplasticity is the brain's lifelong ability to reorganize— to regenerate or to even create anew— its neural pathways based on new information and experiences.

The brain can change positively, known as "positive neuroplasticity," or the brain can change negatively, known as "negative neuroplasticity." Negative neuroplasticity occurs after negative emotional events, trauma, loss, and even abuse. Positive neuroplasticity occurs after healing, positive relationships, and connection.

The SheWorth Journal will prompt you to generate your own innate ability to heal yourself, your thoughts, and your well-being by focusing on gratitude, goal setting, appreciation, and affirmations.

What choices are you making to "change your brain" for the better? WE have the power to change our brains, and that is so empowering. Let this journal guide you in the right direction and witness the transformation.

*Don't mute your real personality.
The world needs more of what
makes you, uniquely you.*

Mirror Neurons

Who you hang out with TRULY does impact who you become. A mirror neuron is a neuron that fires both when an animal acts and when the animal observes the same action performed by another. In other words, we start to emulate and imitate the people whom we spend time with.

Why is this important for you? Because it is essential to understand that in order for you to tune into your intrinsic worthiness, you may need to take a cold, hard look at the relationships in your life and ask yourself:

Are you **Serving** me?

OR

Are you **Depleting** me?

We want to ensure that the mirror neurons in our own brains are around positive people who build us up and make us feel worthy. If anyone does not, it's time to re-think the relationship and take strides toward changing.

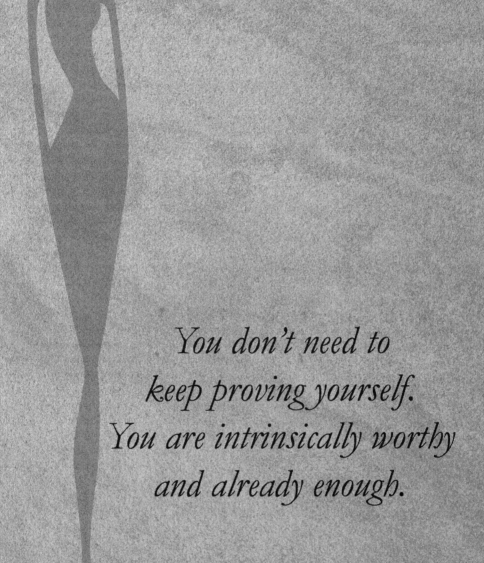

You don't need to
keep proving yourself.
You are intrinsically worthy
and already enough.

Internal Audience

Your "Internal Audience" is a concept from the great Psychologist, Doug Lisle, PhD*. Inside all of us is a "barometer" that is always monitoring and watching whether or not we are living in alignment with the type of person we would like to be.

Do you see yourself as an honest person? A healthy eater? A shy person? A confident person? Whatever your own version of reality is, and whatever values you hold HIGH, are the ways in which you judge yourself.

When we make a choice that confirms our values, our internal audience notices, claps, and we feel good. Perhaps we even feel a surge of a "feel-good" neurotransmitter like Dopamine.

When we do something that goes against our values or that we feel "ashamed of," our internal audience also notices and we feel accordingly.

The point is, you need to know yourself well enough to be able to make choices that are going to signal worthiness to your Internal Audience on a daily basis. It doesn't have to be big, it can be simple like a walk outside, or eating some veggies, or taking an extra moment with your kids. The KEY is, that this internal barometer is incredibly important for your well-being, which is why the SheWorth Journal encourages you to know what impacts your "Internal Audience" positively and to commit to doing something in that direction on a daily basis.

You got this!!!

* Esteemdynamics.org; Doug Lisle, PhD.

You got this girl!
Don't look back.

Positive Psychology

This Journal is based on the principles of Positive Psychology. Why Positive Psychology? Because instead of focusing on what may be wrong, Positive Psychology tries to focus on what is right.

Positive Psychology is the scientific study of the strengths that enable individuals to thrive. The field is founded on the belief that people want to lead meaningful and fulfilling lives, to cultivate what is best within themselves, and to enhance their experiences of love, work, and play.*

By focusing on your strengths rather than on your weaknesses, you can build resilience and confidence within yourself. What are your strengths? How can you use these to show up in your life? SheWorth strives to help women understand how they can live their best life. Using the principles of Positive Psychology allows you to get closer to that outcome.

* Positive Psychology Center, University of Pennsylvania- Martin E.P. Seligman, PhD.

What makes you feel **empowered?**
When do you **feel your best?**
Cultivate more of that and
own your worth.

Negativity Bias

Our brains are wired to notice, encode, and remember the bad. Our brains are NOT as wired to notice, encode, and remember the good.

Why is this? It is for evolutionary reasons. It was VERY important in Stone Age times that we remember where we were when a lion attacked us so that we did not go back and risk our lives again. It was MORE important for our brains to remember dangerous, negative, frightening situations than it was important for our brains to remember neutral, pleasant, or good situations.

The brain is wired to think about the worst case scenario or remember the bad things that have happened to us. It is less inclined to remember the good.

For this reason, it is in our best interest to INTENTIONALLY encode the GOOD! Gratitude practices, in which we notice the good things around us, have long been shown to have positive psychological outcomes. Gratitude practices can send a surge of positive neurotransmitters throughout the body and also help to counter our negativity bias. Gratitude helps to remind us of the good in our life, even when it may be difficult to see during challenging times.

The SheWorth Journal encourages you to retrain the brain so that you can have a more realistic balance of good to bad and encourage your worthiness along the way.

Today and Everyday..
Be **Strong.**
Be **Yourself.**
Be **Independent.**
Be **Ambitious.**
Be **Real.**
Be **Worthy.**

Fixed vs. Growth Mindset

Your mindset can have a profound impact on how you handle challenging situations. The distinction between a fixed and a growth mindset was crystallized by Researcher Carol S. Dweck*. The importance of this distinction is sprinkled throughout the SheWorth Journal so that you do not see your current situation or your past as a determinant of your future. To give you an overview of the difference:

Fixed Mindset:
The belief that your intelligence, creativity, situation or personality is fixed.

Vs.

Growth Mindset:
The belief that your intelligence, creativity, situation, or personality can be developed

The SheWorth Journal encourages you to view situations, circumstances, and past mistakes as learning opportunities and temporary. Failing is simply feedback. We want you to embrace your life and view challenges as opportunities rather than something to be avoided.

*Stanford University- Carol S. Dweck

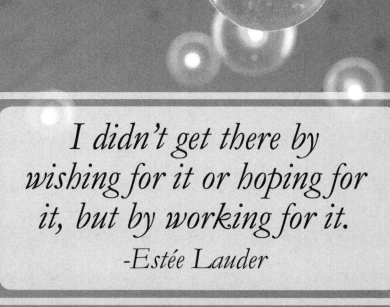

I didn't get there by wishing for it or hoping for it, but by working for it.
-Estée Lauder

Creative Mind Wandering

SheWorth aspires to be a place for you to let your mind wander. So much of our life is spent trying to be "busy" or "productive," at the expense of our brain's ability to come up with creative ideas or insights when it is wandering. We want to encourage creative mind wandering time because the research shows how beneficial it can be.

Recent research has revealed that mind-wandering is a fundamental part of our daily reflection time and its frequency is usually high during relatively easy and low difficulty tasks, while decreasing gradually with increasing task difficulty. These results, although indirect, suggest that a cognitive style characterized by mind-wandering would seem to favor creativity.*

Not only do we believe that it will favor creativity, but it will also favor deepening self-knowledge and clarity for decisions we may be facing. SheWorth wants you to VALUE your creative mind wandering time when you are doing relatively simple tasks such as walking, journaling, or knitting. You may not see this as "valuable," but we beg to differ.

Do your thing. **You are WORTH it!**

No one is going to save you.
Believe in yourself whatever you do,
it comes from you. You are worth it
and can do anything.

Love yourself.

Be less tolerant.
It's OK to disagree and it's OK for
people to not like what you've said.

TRUST YOUR INSTINCTS,

Run !

LISTEN MORE TO YOUR
INTUITION, AND RESPECT
YOURSELF MORE.

It's going to be a rough ride,
but you will make it through.

Choose YOU first.

Don't be afraid to listen to
your own feelings.
Don't always put others
feelings above your own.
You have value and are worth
more.

Don't be so trusting, listen
to what your instincts are
telling you.

You are the most important thing.
No one's needs should come before your own.
You can only love when you can love yourself.

Inspired Words

To your left, you will find a collection of replies from REAL women who were asked "What would your older self say to your younger self?" The women who were asked this question had been in relationships with partners who were NOT worthy of them. All of these women have come out of their relationships and the wisdom collected is meant to inspire you to find your own path to worthiness.

Affirmation Ideas

Today I will remain true to myself. I will honor my feelings.

I release the need to wear masks.

My soul heals through honesty and truthfulness.

It is safe to shine.

I cultivate new hobbies that I enjoy.

My relationships reflect my true values.

I accept myself.

I deserve love and I accept it now.

I practice healthy boundaries in my relationships.

I am skillful at balancing work, play and solitude.

I am worthy.

I nourish my body with health food every day.

I let go of toxic relationships.

I let go of shame and guilt.

I am the most positive person I know.

I accept mistakes as part of being human.

I allow myself to trust in love.

I am an exceptional wife.

I am an exceptional mom.

I am an exceptional human being.

I now free myself from destructive fears and doubts.

I am worth loving. There is love all around me.

I am so strong.

Affirmation Bank

Affirmations, mirror work, and repetition of "I" statements are powerful reminders of where we would like to go. Each day, you will focus on an affirmation. It may be the same for several days or even weeks. If you are struggling for ideas, please reference this page for inspiration!

Section 2
Your Path to Worthiness

An opportunity to quiet your mind and go within every day.
You are worthy.

Date Apil. 24/21

A.M. *How do you feel right now?* ○○○✓○○○○○○
Good   Not Good

Today I commit to...

Doing things that give Me - not
waiting on others to fill the
void in My heart Learn to enjoy
alone time.

The affirmation I will repeat to myself today is...

I release the need to wear
Masks.

Because I am worthy, I will...

jarnal, do things that bring
Me joy - seck nappiness
in Myself, not Hayden

P.M. *How do you feel right now?* ☑○○○○○○○○○
Good   *Not Good*

What is one thing that went well today...

- We had the best w/o session after dinner/steam
- I went to Home sense a felt so excited picking things I liked.
- cleaned/remedied office

Today, I am proud that I...

Got out my negative thinking + didn't let t ruin my day

Tomorrow, I hope to...

Enjoy yoga w the Johnson Fam and enjoy a relaxing spa day — take the rest I deserve!!

☑ *I told myself that I was worthy today.*

37

Date Mon Apr 26 2021

A.M. *How do you feel right now?* ☑️○○○○○○○○○
Good   Not Good

sun right romantic yoga, steam, eat out sesh - best ever on alaskan trip.

Today I commit to...

- Going with the Flow
- Preppin Meals
- grocery Shoppin
- Dancing to great Music w/ Hayden

The affirmation I will repeat to myself today is...

Life is incredible, I am so grateful for the mental + physical "Freeness"

Because I am worthy, I will...

- Spread love to Friends, family + Strangers.
- Realize that I have a voice and sex heals

P.M.

How do you feel right now? ○○○○○○○○○
Good   Not Good

What is one thing that went well today...

....

....

....

....

Today, I am proud that I...

....

....

....

....

Tomorrow, I hope to...

....

....

....

....

☐ *I told myself that I was worthy today.*

A.M. *How do you feel right now?* ○○○○○○○○○
Good *Not Good*

Today I commit to...

....

....

....

....

....

The affirmation I will repeat to myself today is...

....

....

....

Because I am worthy, I will...

....

....

....

....

P.M. *How do you feel right now?* ○○○○○○○○○○
                                        Good   *Not Good*

What is one thing that went well today...

....

....

....

....

Today, I am proud that I...

....

....

....

....

Tomorrow, I hope to...

....

....

....

....

☐ *I told myself that I was worthy today.*

41

A.M.   *How do you feel right now?*   ○○○○○○○○○○
                                       Good   Not Good

Today I commit to...

....

....

....

....

....

The affirmation I will repeat to myself today is...

....

....

....

Because I am worthy, I will...

....

....

....

....

P.M.

How do you feel right now? ○○○○○○○○○
Good   Not Good

What is one thing that went well today...

....

....

....

....

Today, I am proud that I...

....

....

....

....

Tomorrow, I hope to...

....

....

....

....

I told myself that I was worthy today.

A.M. *How do you feel right now?* ○○○○○○○○○○
Good   Not Good

Today I commit to...

....

....

....

....

....

The affirmation I will repeat to myself today is...

....

....

....

Because I am worthy, I will...

....

....

....

....

P.M. *How do you feel right now?*

Good   Not Good

What is one thing that went well today...

....

....

....

....

Today, I am proud that I...

....

....

....

....

Tomorrow, I hope to...

....

....

....

....

☐ *I told myself that I was worthy today.*

45

A.M. *How do you feel right now?* ○○○○○○○○○
Good   Not Good

Today I commit to...

....

....

....

....

....

The affirmation I will repeat to myself today is...

....

....

....

Because I am worthy, I will...

....

....

....

....

P.M.

How do you feel right now? ○○○○○○○○○○
Good   Not Good

What is one thing that went well today...

....

....

....

....

Today, I am proud that I...

....

....

....

....

Tomorrow, I hope to...

....

....

....

....

☐ *I told myself that I was worthy today.*

A.M.   *How do you feel right now?* ○○○○○○○○○○
                                Good   Not Good

Today I commit to...

....

....

....

....

....

The affirmation I will repeat to myself today is...

....

....

....

Because I am worthy, I will...

....

....

....

....

P.M.

How do you feel right now? ○○○○○○○○○

Good   Not Good

What is one thing that went well today...

....

....

....

....

Today, I am proud that I...

....

....

....

....

Tomorrow, I hope to...

....

....

....

....

☐ *I told myself that I was worthy today.*

Date _____

A.M.

How do you feel right now? ○○○○○○○○○
Good   Not Good

Today I commit to...

....

....

....

....

....

The affirmation I will repeat to myself today is...

....

....

....

Because I am worthy, I will...

....

....

....

....

P.M.   *How do you feel right now?*   ○○○○○○○○○○
                                      Good   *Not Good*

What is one thing that went well today...

....

....

....

....

Today, I am proud that I...

....

....

....

....

Tomorrow, I hope to...

....

....

....

....

☐ *I told myself that I was worthy today.*

Date _____

A.M. *How do you feel right now?* ○○○○○○○○○
Good   Not Good

Today I commit to...

....

....

....

....

....

The affirmation I will repeat to myself today is...

....

....

....

Because I am worthy, I will...

....

....

....

....

P.M.

How do you feel right now? ○○○○○○○○○○
Good   Not Good

What is one thing that went well today...

....

....

....

....

Today, I am proud that I...

....

....

....

....

Tomorrow, I hope to...

....

....

....

....

☐ *I told myself that I was worthy today.*

Date _____

A.M. *How do you feel right now?* ○○○○○○○○○
Good   Not Good

Today I commit to...

....

....

....

....

....

The affirmation I will repeat to myself today is...

....

....

....

Because I am worthy, I will...

....

....

....

....

P.M. *How do you feel right now?* ○○○○○○○○○○
Good   *Not Good*

What is one thing that went well today...

....

....

....

....

Today, I am proud that I...

....

....

....

....

Tomorrow, I hope to...

....

....

....

....

☐ *I told myself that I was worthy today.*

A.M. *How do you feel right now?* ○○○○○○○○○
Good   Not Good

Today I commit to...

....

....

....

....

....

The affirmation I will repeat to myself today is...

....

....

....

Because I am worthy, I will...

....

....

....

....

P.M.   *How do you feel right now?*   ○○○○○○○○○○
                                          Good   *Not Good*

What is one thing that went well today...

....

....

....

....

Today, I am proud that I...

....

....

....

....

Tomorrow, I hope to...

....

....

....

....

☐ *I told myself that I was worthy today.*

57

A.M.   *How do you feel right now?*   ○○○○○○○○○
                                          Good   Not Good

Today I commit to...

....

....

....

....

....

The affirmation I will repeat to myself today is...

....

....

....

Because I am worthy, I will...

....

....

....

....

P.M.   *How do you feel right now?* ○○○○○○○○○
                                        Good   Not Good

What is one thing that went well today...

....

....

....

....

Today, I am proud that I...

....

....

....

....

Tomorrow, I hope to...

....

....

....

....

☐ *I told myself that I was worthy today.*

A.M.   *How do you feel right now?*   ○○○○○○○○○
                                          Good   *Not Good*

Today I commit to...

....

....

....

....

....

The affirmation I will repeat to myself today is...

....

....

....

Because I am worthy, I will...

....

....

....

....

P.M.   *How do you feel right now?*   ○○○○○○○○○○
                                        Good   Not Good

What is one thing that went well today...

....

....

....

....

Today, I am proud that I...

....

....

....

....

Tomorrow, I hope to...

....

....

....

....

☐ *I told myself that I was worthy today.*

A.M.   *How do you feel right now?*   ○○○○○○○○○
                          Good   Not Good

Today I commit to...

....

....

....

....

....

The affirmation I will repeat to myself today is...

....

....

....

Because I am worthy, I will...

....

....

....

....

P.M.   *How do you feel right now?* ○○○○○○○○○○
Good   *Not Good*

What is one thing that went well today...

....

....

....

....

Today, I am proud that I...

....

....

....

....

Tomorrow, I hope to...

....

....

....

....

☐ *I told myself that I was worthy today.*

63

A.M. *How do you feel right now?* ○○○○○○○○○
Good   Not Good

Today I commit to...

....

....

....

....

....

The affirmation I will repeat to myself today is...

....

....

....

Because I am worthy, I will...

....

....

....

....

P.M. *How do you feel right now?* ○○○○○○○○○○
Good   *Not Good*

What is one thing that went well today...

....

....

....

....

Today, I am proud that I...

....

....

....

....

Tomorrow, I hope to...

....

....

....

....

☐ *I told myself that I was worthy today.*

Date _____

A.M.   *How do you feel right now?*   ○○○○○○○○○○
                                        Good   Not Good

Today I commit to...

....

....

....

....

....

The affirmation I will repeat to myself today is...

....

....

....

Because I am worthy, I will...

....

....

....

....

P.M. *How do you feel right now?* ○○○○○○○○○
Good   *Not Good*

What is one thing that went well today...

....

....

....

....

Today, I am proud that I...

....

....

....

....

Tomorrow, I hope to...

....

....

....

....

☐ *I told myself that I was worthy today.*

Date _____

A.M. *How do you feel right now?* ○○○○○○○○○○
Good   Not Good

Today I commit to...

....

....

....

....

....

The affirmation I will repeat to myself today is...

....

....

....

Because I am worthy, I will...

....

....

....

....

P.M. *How do you feel right now?* ○○○○○○○○○
Good   *Not Good*

What is one thing that went well today...

....

....

....

....

Today, I am proud that I...

....

....

....

....

Tomorrow, I hope to...

....

....

....

....

☐ *I told myself that I was worthy today.*

A.M. *How do you feel right now?* ○○○○○○○○○
Good   Not Good

Today I commit to...

....
....
....
....

The affirmation I will repeat to myself today is...

....
....
....

Because I am worthy, I will...

....
....
....
....

P.M.

How do you feel right now? ○○○○○○○○○○
Good   *Not Good*

What is one thing that went well today...

....

....

....

....

Today, I am proud that I...

....

....

....

....

Tomorrow, I hope to...

....

....

....

....

☐ *I told myself that I was worthy today.*

71

A.M. *How do you feel right now?* ○○○○○○○○○
Good   Not Good

Today I commit to...

....

....

....

....

....

The affirmation I will repeat to myself today is...

....

....

....

Because I am worthy, I will...

....

....

....

....

P.M.

How do you feel right now? ○○○○○○○○○
Good   Not Good

What is one thing that went well today...

....

....

....

....

Today, I am proud that I...

....

....

....

....

Tomorrow, I hope to...

....

....

....

....

☐ *I told myself that I was worthy today.*

Date _____

A.M. *How do you feel right now?* ○○○○○○○○○
Good   Not Good

Today I commit to...

....

....

....

....

....

The affirmation I will repeat to myself today is...

....

....

....

Because I am worthy, I will...

....

....

....

....

P.M.

How do you feel right now? ○○○○○○○○○○
Good   Not Good

What is one thing that went well today...

....

....

....

....

Today, I am proud that I...

....

....

....

....

Tomorrow, I hope to...

....

....

....

....

☐ *I told myself that I was worthy today.*

A.M. *How do you feel right now?* ○○○○○○○○○
                                        Good   Not Good

Today I commit to...

....

....

....

....

....

The affirmation I will repeat to myself today is...

....

....

....

Because I am worthy, I will...

....

....

....

....

P.M. *How do you feel right now?* ○○○○○○○○○
Good   *Not Good*

What is one thing that went well today...

....

....

....

....

Today, I am proud that I...

....

....

....

....

Tomorrow, I hope to...

....

....

....

....

☐ *I told myself that I was worthy today.*

Date _____

A.M.   *How do you feel right now?*   ○○○○○○○○○
                                        Good   Not Good

Today I commit to...

....

....

....

....

....

The affirmation I will repeat to myself today is...

....

....

....

Because I am worthy, I will...

....

....

....

....

P.M. *How do you feel right now?* ○○○○○○○○○○
Good   Not Good

What is one thing that went well today...

....

....

....

....

Today, I am proud that I...

....

....

....

....

Tomorrow, I hope to...

....

....

....

....

☐ *I told myself that I was worthy today.*

A.M. *How do you feel right now?* ○○○○○○○○○
Good   Not Good

Today I commit to...

....

....

....

....

....

The affirmation I will repeat to myself today is...

....

....

....

Because I am worthy, I will...

....

....

....

....

P.M. *How do you feel right now?* ○○○○○○○○○
Good   *Not Good*

What is one thing that went well today...

....

....

....

....

Today, I am proud that I...

....

....

....

....

Tomorrow, I hope to...

....

....

....

....

☐ *I told myself that I was worthy today.*

81

A.M. *How do you feel right now?* ○○○○○○○○○
Good   Not Good

Today I commit to...

....

....

....

....

....

The affirmation I will repeat to myself today is...

....

....

....

Because I am worthy, I will...

....

....

....

....

P.M.

How do you feel right now? ○○○○○○○○○○
Good   Not Good

What is one thing that went well today...

....

....

....

....

Today, I am proud that I...

....

....

....

....

Tomorrow, I hope to...

....

....

....

....

☐ *I told myself that I was worthy today.*

Date _____

A.M. *How do you feel right now?* ○○○○○○○○○○
Good   Not Good

Today I commit to...

....

....

....

....

....

The affirmation I will repeat to myself today is...

....

....

....

Because I am worthy, I will...

....

....

....

....

P.M.   *How do you feel right now?*   ◯◯◯◯◯◯◯◯◯
                                          Good   *Not Good*

What is one thing that went well today...

....

....

....

....

Today, I am proud that I...

....

....

....

....

Tomorrow, I hope to...

....

....

....

....

☐ *I told myself that I was worthy today.*

85

Date _____

A.M.   *How do you feel right now?*   ○○○○○○○○○
         Good   Not Good

Today I commit to...

....

....

....

....

....

The affirmation I will repeat to myself today is...

....

....

....

Because I am worthy, I will...

....

....

....

....

P.M.

How do you feel right now? ○○○○○○○○○○
Good · Not Good

What is one thing that went well today...

....

....

....

....

Today, I am proud that I...

....

....

....

....

Tomorrow, I hope to...

....

....

....

....

☐ *I told myself that I was worthy today.*

A.M. *How do you feel right now?* ○○○○○○○○○
Good   Not Good

Today I commit to...

....

....

....

....

....

The affirmation I will repeat to myself today is...

....

....

....

Because I am worthy, I will...

....

....

....

....

P.M. *How do you feel right now?* ○○○○○○○○○○
                                      Good   Not Good

What is one thing that went well today...

....

....

....

....

Today, I am proud that I...

....

....

....

....

Tomorrow, I hope to...

....

....

....

....

☐ *I told myself that I was worthy today.*

A.M. *How do you feel right now?* ○○○○○○○○○○
Good   Not Good

Today I commit to...

....

....

....

....

....

The affirmation I will repeat to myself today is...

....

....

....

Because I am worthy, I will...

....

....

....

....

P.M. *How do you feel right now?* ○○○○○○○○○
Good   Not Good

What is one thing that went well today...

....

....

....

....

Today, I am proud that I...

....

....

....

....

Tomorrow, I hope to...

....

....

....

....

☐ *I told myself that I was worthy today.*

Date _____

A.M. *How do you feel right now?* ○○○○○○○○○○
Good   Not Good

Today I commit to...

....
....
....
....

The affirmation I will repeat to myself today is...

....
....
....

Because I am worthy, I will...

....
....
....
....

P.M. *How do you feel right now?* ○○○○○○○○○
Good   *Not Good*

What is one thing that went well today...

....

....

....

....

Today, I am proud that I...

....

....

....

....

Tomorrow, I hope to...

....

....

....

....

☐ *I told myself that I was worthy today.*

Date _____

A.M. *How do you feel right now?* ○○○○○○○○○
Good   Not Good

Today I commit to...

....

....

....

....

....

The affirmation I will repeat to myself today is...

....

....

....

Because I am worthy, I will...

....

....

....

....

P.M. *How do you feel right now?* ○○○○○○○○○
Good   Not Good

What is one thing that went well today...

....

....

....

....

Today, I am proud that I...

....

....

....

....

Tomorrow, I hope to...

....

....

....

....

☐ *I told myself that I was worthy today.*

Section 3
Creativity & Inspiration

*A space for you to dream, aspire, and reflect.
Do not limit yourself or your possibilities.*

You get in life what you have the **Courage** *to ask for.*
Oprah Winfrey

Date: _____

Dream Space
Use this space to dream BIG, let your mind wander, whatever moves you.

Date: _____

Dream Space

Use this space to dream BIG, let your mind wander, whatever moves you.

Dream Space
Use this space to dream BIG, let your mind wander, whatever moves you.

Dream Space

Use this space to dream BIG, let your mind wander, whatever moves you.

Dream Space

Use this space to dream BIG, let your mind wander, whatever moves you.

Date: _____

Dream Space

Use this space to dream BIG, let your mind wander, whatever moves you.

Dream Space

Use this space to dream BIG, let your mind wander, whatever moves you.

Ambition does not mean self-serving, ego-driven, or competitive. These are all cultural constructs that have kept women out of power.

No more.
Know your worth.

*People or scenarios in my life
that build me up...*

*People or scenarios in my life
that deplete me...*

Date: _____

People or scenarios in my life
that build me up...

People or scenarios in my life
that deplete me...

*People or scenarios in my life
that build me up...*

*People or scenarios in my life
that deplete me...*

Date: _____

*People or scenarios in my life
that build me up...*

*People or scenarios in my life
that deplete me...*

People or scenarios in my life
that build me up...

People or scenarios in my life
that deplete me...

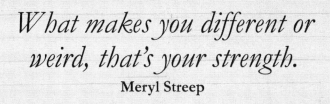

> *What makes you different or weird, that's your strength.*
> **Meryl Streep**

Creative Mind Wandering

Use this space to let your mind wander. Use it not to "solve" a problem, but to let your mind wander on what your emotional state is in this moment.

Date: _____

Creative Mind Wandering

Use this space to let your mind wander. Use it not to "solve" a problem, but to let your mind wander on what your emotional state is in this moment.

Creative Mind Wandering

Use this space to let your mind wander. Use it not to "solve" a problem, but to let your mind wander on what your emotional state is in this moment.

Date: _____

Creative Mind Wandering

Use this space to let your mind wander. Use it not to "solve" a problem, but to let your mind wander on what your emotional state is in this moment.

Creative Mind Wandering

Use this space to let your mind wander. Use it not to "solve" a problem, but to let your mind wander on what your emotional state is in this moment.

Date: _____

Creative Mind Wandering

Use this space to let your mind wander. Use it not to "solve" a problem, but to let your mind wander on what your emotional state is in this moment.

Creative Mind Wandering

Use this space to let your mind wander. Use it not to "solve" a problem, but to let your mind wander on what your emotional state is in this moment.

> *I find that I am much more creative when I've actually taken care of myself.*
>
> **Arianna Huffington**

Goals I am working towards.

Let this space be a place for you to write out 5-10 goals (no matter how big or small) that you are working on right now.

Date: _____

Goals I am working towards.

Let this space be a place for you to write out 5-10 goals (no matter how big or small) that you are working on right now.

Goals I am working towards.

Let this space be a place for you to write out 5-10 goals (no matter how big or small) that you are working on right now.

Date: _____

Goals I am working towards.

Let this space be a place for you to write out 5-10 goals (no matter how big or small) that you are working on right now.

Goals I am working towards.

Let this space be a place for you to write out 5-10 goals (no matter how big or small) that you are working on right now.

You won't find your worth in others. You find your worth in yourself, and then surround yourself with people worthy of you.

Write an encouraging letter to yourself.

Date: _____

Write an encouraging letter to yourself.

Date: _____

Write an encouraging letter to yourself.

If you are not in the arena also getting your ass kicked, I'm not interested in your feedback.

Brene Brown

Brave Moment Zone

Think about times in your life where you felt scared, nervous,
or hesitant. Write about how you made it through.

Date: _____

Brave Moment Zone

*Think about times in your life where you felt scared, nervous,
or hesitant. Write about how you made it through.*

Brave Moment Zone

Think about times in your life where you felt scared, nervous, or hesitant. Write about how you made it through.

Just today... **STOP**
Interrupt the automatic
pattern and see how it feels.
Empowering?

Affirmations Bank

As affirmations change (based on what is going on in your life at that time) put them all in your bank.

Date: _____

Affirmations Bank

As affirmations change (based on what is going on in your life at that time) put them all in your bank.

Affirmations Bank

*As affirmations change (based on what is going on in your life
at that time) put them all in your bank.*

Date: _____

Create!

Date: _____

Reflect

Date: _____

You Got it, Girl!

Date: _____

Be Brave

Strong

Date: _____

You Are Worthy

Section 4
Random Musings

Utilize this lined space as a place to journal your thoughts, ideas, and inspirations. Everyday is a new day to be more authentically you.

Section 4

Section 4

Section 4

You GOT THIS!

Thank You

Thank you for partaking in the SheWorth Journal. Please keep this sacred Journal and reflect back on it with the passage of time. As time passes and you evolve, we hope that this will serve as a snapshot of where you were and of how far you have come.

Please share this with any other amazing women in your life who may need a beautiful place to collect their thoughts and move toward empowerment and healing

With so much Love + Peace,

SheWorth

If you would like more support and inspiration around all things SheWorth, please stay connected to us. We hope to be a place to help you grow, evolve, heal, and change. You are Worth it.

IG: SheWorth_Women
Twitter: @WorthShe
www.sheworth.org